The Darkest Corner

Mark Elliott Fults

Copyright © 2018 Mark Elliott Fults
All rights reserved.
ISBN-9781726867719

CONTENTS

Foreword
Acknowledgments
Preface
History of Dolls
My Concepts

1 Anatoly Moskvin 17

2 Carl Tanzler 24

3 Frozen Charlotte 27

4 Marquis Francesco Longhi 31

5 La Pascualita 33

6 Grave Robbing and the Wax Anatomical Doll 34

7 Robert the Doll 36

8 Shabti Doll 38

9 L'Inconnue de la Seine and the CPR Doll 39

10 Voodoo Doll 41

11 Luk Thep Doll 45

12 Nagoro, Japan 47

13 Isla de las Munecas (The Island of the Dolls) 48

14 Ghost Marriages 49

About the Author

References

Foreword

Dolls, every little girl's dream to have, right? Maybe. Maybe not. Growing up, I collected dolls from all over the world. My parents would bring them back to me from their travels, and their friends would even send me dolls from many different places. I had dolls from all over Europe, Mexico, several different islands, and the Kasba in Africa. When I was older and got to go places on my own, I brought home dolls from Germany, England, Japan and special ones from the states. I had them for many years - some I still have.

But when I was very young and until I reached the age of around 12, I had a problem with dolls: I felt them watching me - so much so, that I had to turn them all around, especially when I dressed. Silly? It wasn't to me at that time. It wasn't until many years later, the more I was involved in paranormal studies, that I became aware there were other people that had similar feelings around dolls.

As you read the following stories, my insecurities may seem a bit more plausible. At least the dolls I collected were toys, right? Or did some (or all) of them have a spirit attached? I may never know, but I do know the feeling I got every time I was near my dolls.

Step inside now and read these stories. Perhaps you can shed some light into The Darkest Corner.

Cyn Shrader Hill

Acknowledgments

I would like to acknowledge my friends who assisted me in weaving this wicked web of disturbing and totally disgusting stories of true events.

First of all, I'd like to thank Cyn Shrader Hill for being brave enough to edit this collection of darkness. It has taken longer to put together because it grossed both of us out severely on several accounts so thank you Cyn for sticking with me on this twisted journey.

Next, I would like to thank Teal Gray from Teal Gray Worldwide and my partner in crime in Gray Fults Press, without whom these books would not be possible.

Next in line is Cynthia Brundage a dear friend for 22 years who did the fabulous cover of this book, as well as my Chattanooga, chills series. Thank you for doing artwork that will help give other people nightmares- couldn't do it without you.

As a lifelong psychic I would like to thank the spirits that assist me in my endeavors. To help find beauty and healing in the midst of terror in the modern world. I always hope to do justice to those I serve.

To the victims in this book you have my heart and soul, and hopefully, I did justice for you in the segments that I speak to spirit. I hope the events that created the stories are something you can move past and find peace in the universal consciousness.

To the monsters that inhabit these pages, I hope what I'm doing will ignite activism to deter stories like this from happening in the future. Hopefully, the evil that has been done will in some way inspire others to stop and prevent predators such as yourselves from being able to destroy lives the way that you have.

To all those who read the stories within these pages beware, you will never be the same ever again. So, as I say in my other books, it is time to part the dark veil and sleep no more...

Preface

the storms of life are over now

maybe I can rest

wrapped up in a satin cloud

nestled in the Earth's brown breast

I want you I need you

but it's over now

I love you I need you

but it's all for the best

somehow

Death: something that is certain for all living things, the end of all for most. To breathe to live is to die. There is a spring or fall followed by winter; then like seeds, we lay buried, most never to see the light again, some dug up to blossom into a new bloom. For me, I believe that once we go beyond the human frailties that we all share and shed this chrysalis, then our energy goes forth and goes toward more. I am a 55-year-old spiritualist witch well into my croning years. I was inspired to write this book after coming across a shocking yet fascinating story: Anatoly Moskvin *The Russian Doll Man*. It haunted me for days, and in the process of trying to process the complexities of shock and horror while I was reading, I saw other issues that were at work.

Here was a man about 45 years old considered to be a genius, able to speak 13 languages and was the expert cemetery historian. He worked at a paper, had a fairly regular life on the surface, but he had a hobby. He collected the corpses of 26 young girls from the age of 3 to 15, stealing them from their graves, and then turned them into dolls. Apparently, he knew all of their birthdays, and he celebrated with parties. He sat and watched cartoons with them. He placed music boxes in their rib cages so that they could *sing* to him and he sang back. When it was exposed that he had these corpses strewn about his apartment they filmed it and put it on live TV.

There are many interpretations of death in Russian folk tradition. It can be reversible, and it sometimes resides outside of the body. It is also closely related to sleep. It is believed that when one sleeps, one can traverse the "other world" and come back alive. There are two kinds of deaths. A person who dies in his or her old age surrounded by family died a *good* death, a death that was *their own*. They depart when God says they should. A person who experiences a *bad* death, or an end *not their own* (died too soon before the time God assigned them). These persons might have been murdered, committed suicide, succumbed to illness, or perished in war. Because of the nature of these deaths, the earth cannot accept them until their time comes which means they do not receive a proper burial and are sometimes not buried at all but covered with rocks or sticks. Russians associate good deaths with bringing good harvests while attributing storms, droughts and other forms of destruction to bad deaths.

Several steps are taken once a person has died so their body can be buried and their soul can travel to the *other world*. First, the body is washed then dressed in all-white, handmade clothing left slightly unfinished because it belongs not in this world but the other world. After preparing the body, it is laid out in the house for three days before being put in the coffin. Orthodox families lay their dead loved one, so his or her head points towards the corner altar. In the houses of Old Believers, the feet are placed closer to the altar so the deceased faces the corner and can pray if he or she desires. Old Believers believe that the dead can still feel for a time after their death. For fear of waking the newly dead, mourning does not begin during the washing or dressing. Inappropriate funeral etiquette can also wake the dead.

The coffin sometimes referred to as the *new living room*, is very comfortable, made like a bed with a pillow stuffed with birch bark or wood shavings. Mourners place objects in the coffin that the body might need after death such as money, food, personal belongings, and reflections of status or occupation. Traditionally, men carry the coffin on their backs to the cemetery where the funeral will take place. At the funeral, a priest performs the *seeing off* ceremony, praying over the body and allowing mourners to throw dirt on the grave, symbolically incorporating the corpse into the earth. The priest then places a paper crown on the head of the deceased, and the mourners throw soil and coins into the grave (the coins are either to pay for transit to the other world or for the space in the cemetery). After the funeral, mourners sing laments depicting the deceased leaving his or her family and the soul departing from the body. Also, it is important to them that any handkerchiefs used to wipe away tears at the funeral are thrown away because it is believed that if you take them home, you are bringing tears into the house.

Olga Chardymova had been murdered at the age of 10 in horrific circumstances about which you will be reading shortly. Her parents received a disturbing phone call that would send their lives into the deepest layers of hell. The police told them about the discovery in Moskvin's apartment and that they had to exhume Olga to be sure she was in her grave. The next day, ironically three days after the 10th anniversary of her burial, they uncovered her casket. It was in good condition for being interred for ten years except there had been a hole cut in the top and Olga had been removed. The grave the family had been visiting to pray and suffer over had been empty for nine years. They knew nothing of the strange man that had mistreated them over the years by secretly stealing their precious only daughter. One of the most chilling things he ever said to them and the other parents of the children he had acquired was that he held them responsible; saying *they had abandoned their girls in the dark, and that he had taken them home and warmed them up.*

The story is perplexing and unimaginable, and to me, Olga is the face of and the poster child depicting a victim of necrophilia and necromancy. My maternal and paternal instincts came raging to the surface. Initially, seeing this beautiful child's pre-death photos, my first instinct was to protect this fragile little thing by reaching out to save her and all of these children, but then the realization hits you: there's nothing you can do because they have already met death; they are beyond reach. The families have been destroyed, and then a stranger felt he had the right to desecrate the most sacred of places: the graves of so many children. And not only did Moskvin take those children, he re-created them; besides being a necrophiliac, he was also a necromancer and believed that through science or black magic he could bring these girls back to life.

As I studied this case, looking more at the magical aspect Moskvin, I began discovering multiple modern stories of necrophilia and necromancy; several accounts are within the last 20 years. As a psychic working in the mundane and metaphysical community, I began to look at these stories in a different way. First of course with shock and horror because the perpetrators are monsters; second, the victims who were specific in their details; third, the families and how they reacted and survived; and finally, I looked at it from my psychic experience. I do spiritualist techniques, seances with channeling and remote viewing, and have assisted behind the scenes on murder cases. I have an intense desire to help the victims because I know very well what it is to be a victim of violence.

I also know the 1930's story of Carl Tanzler and his patient Elena that was considered a love story, but he did the same thing that Anatoly Moskvin did to the little girls. The list goes on and on, and I believe that by putting the stories together, I can show a very bizarre part of the human psyche. In my conversations with friends I've brought up some of these issues that they had never thought of, and neither had I.

I have a personal story of someone that I had to deal with just a few years ago: a man plotting to rob the grave of a 10-year-old boy, so he could keep the body and pretend it was his son. I tried multiple times to stop him, but he finally got into trouble for something else, and that ended his attempts. Disturbingly, he is free again, and those in the legal system know he's a violent pedophile but can do nothing until he acts on his tendencies. He will most likely do very bad things causing someone to mourn the death of a child one day, but there is nothing that can be done until he commits something terrible. Sometimes that mindset allows horrendous actions to take place.

Please keep an open mind and remember for us this is fascinatingly shocking, sort of like a car wreck from which you can't walk away. We can look at it, read it, be shocked by it, possibly entertained by it, and then we can walk away from it. We can close the book, turn off our Kindle app, or turn off the laptop and go to bed. The parents and families of the individuals who were stolen or violated cannot shut the book. I doubt they can close their eyes. The parents of those 26 dead, young Russian girls had to deal with and still must endure the horrible loss; but when you think it couldn't get worse, they discover some stranger took the bodies creating the idea that they are 'his children.' Their lives are destroyed further by knowing they could not protect their daughters even in death - survivor's guilt is monstrous, and I do not know how they had the strength to live but they do against all the odds, so remember them and all the victims of murder and foul play. After all the horrible things that life could do to someone, the one thing a person deserves is a respectful death instead of becoming the plaything of a warped individual.

During the 1800s, the young child Marquise Francesco Longhi was killed by his seven sisters, and the parents' sorrow knew no depths. They could not bear to part with their five-year-old son, so they preserved his tiny body and kept him for the rest of their lives placed in a glass container in their bedroom. I heard the story of the father talking to and caressing his son's body acting like he was still alive. There's a ghost story of the mother who comes to weep at the child's container, and there are even stories of the little boy's ghost pulling pranks. The five-year-old's body, the cherub frozen in time with the wax mask preserving his charms as much as possible, lies forever in eternal sleep - a true sleeping beauty. He's on exhibit for anyone to see the results of his terrible death and a sad reminder of his parents who were so heartbroken they could not bear to lose their baby to the earth and the worm. The story is odd but sweetly sad in a tragic way, and they weren't taking someone who didn't love them or have love towards them like a stranger holding a corpse hostage in a fantasy of perceived love. I hope we can see our dead with genuine love and respect.

A few of the cases in this book are odd or bizarre like the previous one which was done without malevolent intent, others are pure evil. In some, no one was harmed when alive, and no one was murdered; instead, the individual took a dead body clutching it as a childhood doll or manikin, but if the individual does harm towards the families then his actions are as evil as those stories you will read about in the second and third books of my trilogy (due out in early 2019). Now, let's look at a brief history of dolls.

History of Dolls

Dolls are representations of us: they have our faces and bodies, hands and feet. In the modern world, they're basically just toys, though extremely detailed and sometimes stylized, that represent every aspect of human life in miniature. There are costumes for different jobs, careers, or occasions, along with houses, cars, appliances, and even pets, and are a mirror reflection of us. Today, they are made primarily of plastic and are fashion dolls representing teenagers and adults. When I was young, there were mostly baby dolls, young girl and teenage dolls. When *Barbie* was introduced, the first modern doll with breasts, she was advertised as an adolescent doll but was really seen as a full-grown woman doll. Some dolls are produced as educational tools, from teaching how to tie bows and buckle shoes, to show where everything in the human body is in order to cut into an individual for surgery correctly.

The most ancient recorded dolls are called *paddle dolls* which were found in Egypt; and around 100 AD in Greece, there's documentation of toy dolls. Over the years there have been many examples of dolls from the very primitive (rag dolls, stiff figures, and a few with jointed arms and legs) all the way up to those produced as exquisite art forms. Nowadays most people don't realize that in the ancient world, the vast majority of dolls were not toys; they were a part of religious ritual which included magical purposes. They could represent a person and their health or status and could be used to heal or to kill in a ritualistic manner. Some dolls were and are embedded and may be too magical to be considered toys.

In some parts of the world, the figure represents a family member - an ancestor - treated with respect and is passed down to be taken care of through the family. In African cultures sometimes, the doll would be an effigy to do magic upon an individual; this has evolved in the modern world through witchcraft and folk practices including Voodoo which is so prevalent - everyone knows what a voodoo doll is.

The modern doll can be traced back to 15th century Germany. Soon after, in Paris, figures were created to be fashion models or ambassadors of style. The latest clothing would be designed in miniature, placed on the dolls, and sent all across Europe to show the styles offered. These dolls were expensive and were not made as toys, but many of them ended up in the hands of the children of those who received the dolls; it showed there could be a doll market aimed at children. In Europe and then after the Civil War in America, there became a large booming business: china dolls were created by the millions to be purchased by little girls or for little girls. In this book, among many other things, I will speak about my grandmother's dolls. The materials most popular for the ones she had were bisque (which she called *biscuit dolls*), china, and porcelain.

Through the years dolls have been made from clay, wood, leather, ivory or bone, stone, papier-mâché, porcelain, wax, plastic, cloth, paper, composition (a mixture of paper, sawdust, plaster, and glue), and other materials such as cornhusks and apples. While in my first coven, I remember creating kitchen witch dolls for good luck. I have also made dolls out of corn cobs and apples. Apple head dolls are actually very fascinating; once you carve the fruit, it shrinks as it dehydrates and takes on the appearance of a very old person.

When I was very young, three and four years old, I played with dolls, and I was a very isolated child until I was about five. The toy that I was given was my only friend at that time because I wasn't exposed to other children except for my siblings. That doll became as real a friend as an actual living person. Just before I turned five, my family decided they needed to take the doll way from me, so they did so while I was sleeping. When I awoke, I looked for my friend and didn't understand where she could be. I looked for her a very long time. My family was embarrassed that I played with dolls as a little boy or a transgender child, and they treated me differently as if something was wrong with me. Typically, the children who play with dolls tend to be more nurturing, as I have become.

I have a lifelong fascination with dolls, and as a metaphysical person, it is understood that these figures are more than a mirror image; they can be a vessel for energy, hold consciousness, and be a thinking entity if embedded correctly. The doll on the cover of this book, a wax over papier-mâché doll from the 1870s or 1880s, is one of those; she has energy that was embedded into her years ago, and she still emits feelings. The general response she evokes is a wish to protect her. She is perfect for the cover because not only do I wish to protect her, I want to protect all the children in this book.

I have come into contact with possessed dolls, some that were frightening, and some that were heart-wrenching. In your travels when you see antique dolls, try to assess the feeling that they project. Not all dolls have a spirit in them or a consciousness, but for the ones that do, try to see what they are conveying, and you may find there's more than meets the eye. If you collect antique dolls, treat them kindly because you never know when one will surprise you; but beware: if you have one in your home that has ill will or has been used in magic, you may never sleep again.

My Concept

I have had to deal with human frailties all my life. I was born with Marfan Syndrome, a genetic disorder that affects the body's connective tissue holding all the cells, tissues and organs together. At the age of 30, I was viciously attacked in a random act of violence. My arm, shoulders, and hip were dislocated, and I suffered several fractured ribs, a collapsed lung and all of my organs were knocked loose from the lining. The damage was so extensive that I had two near-death experiences in the hospital. I could have been dead, buried and rotting in a box for 25 years dressed in an ugly polyester suit in which my mother would've put me; instead, I have had this time to live life, and for some reason I have something to offer, so I'm trying to do as much as possible.

My intent in life is to help and to educate. I try to live my life backward, forwards, and side to side. I have been psychic since at least four when I had my first real experience, but other people noticed when I was around the age of six. At 18, I joined a Wiccan group and developed my skills as an energy technician through discipline. Everything revolves around energy - everything. The unseen things around us exist, but they are just that - unseen. You cannot see the air (unless you're in California) but it is there nonetheless, and once you don't have it you realize how important it is and how real it is - It exists whether we think about it or not. In many ways, I believe the spirit is like that. Our energy exists whether we believe in it or not, and that essence is nothing more and nothing less than miraculous.

In my upcoming book, *The Psychic Worm Stitch*, I will explain the world according to Mark, how I feel it works and how I, as a psychic, function within these electromagnetic bands we call dimensions. But here I'm just touching on some of my beliefs so that when I discuss trying to contact any spirit involved in these circumstances, it will allow you to follow my working process.

My skills have come about after 37 years of discipline, education and sheer willpower. To begin explanation: each person has an aura. When we are born, we contain a sliver of core energy that has been recycled from a self-regulatory system called Earth. Most people consider that center to be the 'spirit energy' and it is almost like a radioactive material inserted into your physical form through the birth process. Everything is connected, and everything has some of the same energy you have in your core; it is part of an ancient force that has been purified, recycled and has through process become the center of the being. While you are living, this energy coming from your center creates through frequency your aura, which for most radiates about 18 to 24 inches away from the person (a sphere around the body). Chakras are energy centers that are aligned from the top of your head down through the body. The soul energy is old and contains information. Your physical self has DNA from hundreds of thousands of people not only recording hair, eye, and skin color but also talents and skills which is how people inherit skills of singing, artwork and other talents biologically. Along with physical makeup and ability, the DNA contains memory, so you are born with the intuitive memory of anyone who added to your DNA pool in the process of reproduction. The energies and memories of your soul are separate from the ones ingrained in your body; then as you (the new person) grow and learn, you create the personality that is you (the current person).

Your spirit is an electromagnetic plasma that records and conveys, and your brain working during waking hours as well as while sleeping can hold about 3 million hours of information that never goes away. From birth until death, once any energy in your body is expelled, such as thought waves, your electromagnetic plasma records each second of it. When your body dies the electromagnetic plasma-shell, your spirit, is still functioning and vibrating and separates from the physical self as it is pulled magnetically to specific dimensional levels that are drawn towards each other. Our energy which cannot be destroyed, transitions into a different form and downloads into the dimensional layers of the self-regulating Earth. Anything that has ever been thought, acted upon, or felt is a vibration, and the energy in it is still in existence somewhere in the invisible substance in which we function. So, if you follow this idea and can understand the dimensional fields, you can then track specific energy that is recorded in the universe by magnetizing it to you.

The aura that you are emitting is like a CAT scan that can be trained as your personal type of energy virus protection. We get 'gut' feelings that are projected by all individuals, and each of us can be infected by other energies just as a computer gets a virus, so creating a spherical boundary encapsulating your aura is important. As an energy technician, a witch and psychic, I am taught to control and set up boundaries to control the exchange of energy and information. During work, if something is not good for your energy, you can expel that foreign energy by keeping your boundary strong and the frequency of your aura at a high level. When something is invasive, you raise your frequency, and because you have a boundary, it burns it out of your system. Once you have control of that system as a psychic, you can use your frequency which is in a controlled container to communicate with other spheres of energy that we call 'spirits.'

When you die the mineral-based physical form stops functioning, and it becomes cold and heavier because it is no longer emitting energy. Although the body dies, the electromagnetic plasma frequency (an exact electrical copy of the body) is still functioning and vibrates at an even higher level. The spirit separates from the body through this vibration and is pulled through electromagnetic energy bands. These bands growing outward are drawn into the atmosphere from the center of the equator towards each pole of the earth.

As the spirit is pulled it fluctuates and creates bands of energy, and between these bands are walls of energy. The walls are a living fabric which we call the 'veil.'

There are two times of the year when the veil increases as the old falls away a little, pulling and separating, and the new layer of the veil energy emerges; just like tree bark when the new bark comes from underneath and the upper layer becomes the bark on the outside. The material of the veil is a vibrating string-like material. When it is pulled it can tear (but is not really tearing it is just vibrating apart as it stretches, and when the material is relaxed it vibrates back into place). By using pinpoint accuracy, you can make the veil separate and obtain frequencies through the material, allowing communication with information that exists within the dimensional channels.

As a psychic consider me an antique ham radio. I have a frequency that I raise after using a disciplined technique to prepare my aura, and I can pick up a specific frequency or sphere of energy (someone else's spirit) with which I wish to communicate. One reason psychics have people bring them item's that belong to a deceased person is that that item has specific energy codes of the individual who owned it and embedded into the article. A psychic can take that item and use it as a metal detector. Each spirit has an energy trail that it leaves automatically inserted into the invisible material of the universe around us. Energy cannot be destroyed. There is always an essence trail or tether that can lead to the specific sphere of energy, namely the spirit of the person who is now deceased. Their electromagnetic plasma, if following the natural process, is drawn to certain levels of dimensional energy that is magnetized at the same frequency.

Different things can disrupt this process because the spirit is separate from the personality. When we talk about the spirit going 'to the light,' this is on a cellular level and in reality, is the light of our dying neurons which are brighter as they shoot off. When a spirit sees the light, their energy downloads into it through the neuron's nucleus which then processes through the pineal gland (the third eye) further downloading into a universal dimensional energy layer. From there, the spirit goes on into whatever level of the universal brain that it is going to, or what we consider the Afterlife.

Now if the personality is strong enough to overcome the natural process, then it can create a 'discarnate spirit.' The personality that is you in this life can be so focused on staying, that it disrupts the natural process causing the spirit to function around the life it used to have: around the people, the circumstances, or any areas in which it lived. Eventually, these disruptions are called hauntings and can continue for quite a while. Because they are energy, some spirits learn how to feed themselves from any form of energy surrounding the area including thermal, electrical, and mineral, and can exist quite a while on their own. Eventually, if they do not learn how to feed, the spirit's electromagnetic plasma thickens and congeals because it is no longer emitting a viable higher frequency.

The spirit goes back into the center and takes all that information with it that has been recorded.

Your spirit will learn things while it is living and carry that information back with it to the core; similar to going to school and then graduating; you take the information and knowledge you acquired and go to the next level. So, when I tune my frequency to a specific spirit, I fine-tune my energy levels and then I use an antique spiritualist call to speak to the personality and spirit within that sphere of information. A ghost can be the complete spirit of the individual that has passed, or it can be the personality and the recorded data from the life of that individual. Through energy techniques, I can communicate with that spirit and receive encoded information from it, or if it speaks consciously, I can directly communicate with the spirit.

Now let's see if we can't peek behind this cloudy veil that others are reaching through and beyond to break the bonds of mortality and attempt to bring life back into a desiccated corpse. I want the psychic ability issues to enhance the conversation, not detract. You can skip my observations and just read the stories I'm going to present to you because they reach beyond fantasy and science fiction. These events occurred, and they continue to happen. In my psychic attempts, I hope to do justice for the spirits of these innocent beings who need to be protected even in death.

I, the psychic, try to look at the dead differently. Do I believe the deceased has gone or is there a consciousness still attached to the body through an energy tether? Maybe the deceased is unable to find relief from its woes or to attempt to communicate with their family and friends so that they know the condition of their loved one. Or is the body merely an empty vessel which the spirit has moved beyond the reach of humankind?

In all of these cases in this book, even though there is a spiritual aspect, no one has attempted to analyze or contact spirits of these victims, and that is what I plan to address. As I said before, I am an energy technician and spirits are energy. I will explain how I function and how we can look at what's possibly happening from the other side. Some of these necrophiliacs professed love for these strangers, taking the corpses using them as blank slates projecting their fantasies upon them and convincing themselves they were doing something lovely. So, bear with me, and I will lead you through the stories, breaking them down in the way I see them. You do not have to believe in psychics to read this book nor need any preconceived notions; as a matter of fact, I hope you will look at this information several times and break it down yourself, looking at it in many different ways (social implications, personal applications, and warning signs). There are things that these predators did along the way that could've stopped these horrible outcomes, but people chose to ignore everything and not to get involved. We need to assess who we are and what they are.

So now our journey begins. Be brave because the world we are about to explore will take us into the farthest reaches of the darkest corners of the human psyche. All we can do is pray that we do not succumb to the dark nature ourselves searching for our love beyond the grave. Here we go beyond the veil of reason and light...

Anatoly Moskvin

Anatoly Yurevych Moskvin (Russian: born Sept. 1, 1966) of Nizhny Novgorod, Russia, a renowned as a brilliant historian of graveyards and cemeteries, was also a purveyor of one of the most perverted incidences in modern history. Anatoly was arrested in 2011 after twenty-six mummified bodies of girls aged three to fifteen were found in the apartment he shared with his parents.

Moskvin used Celtic techniques to speak to the dead, lying on the grave attempting to converse with the little girl's spirit entombed there. He told about hearing the little girl's voice asking him to "take (her) for a walk," upon which he would dig up the body and hide it in the cemetery while he mummified it. He used a mixture of salt, baking soda, and homemade remedies to dry out the body. Anatoly would then carry the body home covering it in many layers of stocking and fabric such as silk or gauze dipped in wax - much like Carl Tanzler had done to his obsession, Elena - turning her into a large plaster doll, hoping to one day bring her (and the rest of them) back to life using science or black magic. He conveyed he felt the girls wouldn't want to come back to life in ugly bodies, so he covered them in fabric and painted faces on some, but others were left unpainted. Moskvin would then put music boxes between the girl's ribs so she could *sing* to him. He knew the birth and death dates of each child. It is believed Moskvin disturbed the graves of about 150 girls, but only 26 made it to his apartment.

Anatoly remembered his fascination with death began as a small child, telling the story of a close friend, a little girl, who died at age eleven. At her funeral "an adult pushed my face down to the waxy forehead of the girl in an embroidered cap, and there was nothing I could do but kiss her as ordered."

I know from the stories I heard my family tell, that forcing a child to kiss a corpse is a traumatic experience. When my maternal great-grandfather died in 1902, an uncle forced my grandmother, Granny Swearingen, a crying child, to kiss her father's brow. She told me it was a horrifying event and one that disturbed her for the rest of her life. Victorians here in America forced children to kiss corpses as a regular practice, seeing it as a respectful gesture, but it was discontinued early in the 1900's.

Moskvin became fascinated by death, Celtic burial rituals, and the occult, considering himself a *necropolist*. In his adult life, he was known as a genius who could speak thirteen languages, an owner of 60,000 books and documents, a virgin who abstained from alcohol and drugs, as well as a man who never dated anyone, never married, and always lived with his parents.

In 2005, Anatoly was hired to make a list of the dead in forty regions of the Nizhny Novgorod Oblast. He claimed to have inspected 752 cemeteries over a two-year period, walking several miles a day, drinking from puddles and spending nights in barns, or sleeping in the graveyards themselves. He reported having even slept one night in a coffin that was being prepared for a funeral. Although police sometimes questioned him on suspicion of vandalism and theft, he was never arrested during that two-year period. Apparently, the officials fell for his story of investigating cemeteries as a historian, which was true, but he was much more than that.

Moskvin was arrested on November 2, 2011, by police investigating several grave desecrations. As a matter of fact, the authorities came to him as an expert to see if he could help them with any leads, but they soon realized something darker was going on with Anatoly. Investigators from the Center for Combating Extremism discovered bodies in Moskvin's apartment and released a video showing the *dolls* arranged on furniture, lying on the floor, and stuffed into piles of books, paper, and trash. His parents who were away most of the time each year had seen the mummies but had thought they were just part of his hobby of making dolls, unaware each one contained a body of a little girl. Among his papers and books, the police found metal nameplates removed from headstones, instructions for making the *dolls*, maps of the cemeteries, along with videos and photographs of open graves and bodies.

Anatoly was charged with the desecration of graves and dead bodies carrying up to five years in prison, but after a psychiatric evaluation, it was determined that Moskvin suffered from a form of paranoid schizophrenia, and in May 2012, he was deemed unfit to stand trial releasing him from criminal liability. He is currently in a psychiatric clinic which reviews his status regularly, and so far, every request for the extension of Moskvin's treatment has been approved.

After his arrest, Moskvin explained that he had learned the ancient Druids and Yakuts had slept on graves to commune with spirits of their dead. He then began searching for recently dead children, and when he found an obituary that *spoke* to him, he would sleep on her grave waiting to hear if the child's spirit wished to be brought back to life. As it became more difficult for him to sleep outside in the weather, he started carrying the bodies home where it would be more comfortable to sleep near them. He also hoped the spirits would be more willing to speak there and it would be easier for him to hear them as they were no longer six feet underground.

Moskvin claimed to have been aware that he was committing a crime but said the dead children were *calling out* to him, begging to be rescued and taken home, which, to him, was more important than obeying the law. Anatoly claimed he had been doing this for about twenty years and denied ever digging up a grave without the permission of the child buried there. He denied ever having sex with the corpses or *dolls*, considering them to be his children.

He was raped as a child and considered sex disgusting. Moskvin had wanted children of his own and at one time attempted to adopt a young girl against the wishes of his parents, but his application was declined because he was single and poor.

He knew each child's birthday from their gravestones or obituaries and would have a party for each one treating them as living children. He would talk to and interact with the corpses, singing songs, watching cartoons and would even celebrate all the holidays with them. Moskvin was angry at the parents of each child believing they had abandoned their children leaving them in the cold graves; he had great animosity towards the families and unleashed his anger upon them torturing them for years. One of the most chilling things he said against the parents of all his *dolls* was that *they had abandoned their girls in the dark, and that he had taken them home and warmed them up.*

Olga Chardymova (Russian: 1992-Oct. 2, 2002) - Anatoly's most famous *doll*.

This is Olga's story before Moskvin took her. When little Olga Chardymova, a beautiful happy child, was just ten years old, she insisted on being able to leave the apartment by herself for the first time. She wanted to show she was a "big girl" by walking to Grandma's house on her own but she never made it there. A drug dealer who lived in her building forced her to the top floor and robbed her of her earrings, and when she tried to escape, he hit her with a metal bar. Her body was then hidden in the attic walls of the building and not found for six months. Her parents had been through hell wondering what had happened; then when Olga's body was found, they were unable to have an open casket to say goodbye to their daughter. Afterward, within months, she was dug up and turned into a *doll* in Anatoly Moskvin's collection held captive for nine years before he was discovered and arrested.

Olga Chardymova Psychic Conversation

On April 18, 2017, after 36 hours of energy preparation, I composed myself to find the correct frequency to communicate with Olga. Because of the circumstances that she experienced I decided to approach her similarly to the way a psychologist speaks with a patient. I always keep an open mind because I do not know in what state the spirit or personality will be: whether it is still troubled, feels endangered or discarded, trapped, fully functional or if it processed naturally and gone on into the light (the processing center). The only way to understand that is through communication. I also put aside any preconceived notions I have concerning everything I've researched about the victim and the situation.

So, I've done my communication techniques, raised my energy and then performed my spiritual call. Each person's energy is distinct, and because of my preparations, my system and powers that assist me are prepared to reach out to this particular individual. When I put out the call to Olga, amazingly I got a response very quickly. Now without bias, I just talk to her as a person. The spirit speaks in frequency and energy levels, so besides verbal, it can communicate telepathically or intuitively which spans any language barrier.

When I called Olga, the response was very clear. First of all, I can say this is a very bright and charming spirit; happy, loving and kind of a sweetly mischievous rascal. When I opened communication, she began to download information about for what I was searching. She does not recall very much about her transitioning experience which we would refer to as her murder. She remembers trying to get away and then she 'woke up' as spirit. She would have followed the natural process into the light, but she felt her parents needed her and she could not just leave them. Because of this, the man she knows as 'Toly' was able to corral her energy through ritual, so she became trapped for a period of time. Only about four of the other 'girls' were trapped similarly; the rest had been able to process and were out of reach. She acted as a big sister to some of the other energies. Her assessment of the experience once past the shock was that even though it was distasteful, it became the regular day to day experience, but she was still very embarrassed to be forced into the situation. She worried about her parents, and she didn't know how to disconnect to get away from the strange man (she would have naturally been able to escape when he died because his energy field would not be able to hold the spirits there).

Olga considers her time with Moskvin as being corralled. She first thought he was a weirdo. She was not amused by the clothes he dressed her in because the pieces of clothing were for a six or seven-year-old child. She did not approve in any way of how he made her look. She was irritated at the paint job on her face he did thinking it terribly crude and just very unnerving. She felt the games he played were boring and for someone much younger, so she had no interest in sitting around for them. The cartoons he showed were not any that she cared for, and she conveyed "my mother would never have allowed me to live in a such a nasty dirty home. He was just a mess."

The reason some of the other 'girls' were placed in the garage and under things was they did not have the spirit in them, so he lost interest. He could tell the ones that vibrated energy and kept them in the apartment. Olga continued "He is not my father and not my mother; he is just a strange experience. Once we were taken out of that situation, then his energy hold on us was broken. My grandmother assisted me in getting in line, and I now move freely. I check on my family every day. I watch over my brother because he's frail or fragile in a way. I am trying to comfort my parents, but I know they just don't know I'm there; they know, but they don't know. The things I missed while I was in 'the flat': animals, drawing pictures, but mostly my family. I was extremely bored. Now I am in my 20s, but I understand I will always be a little girl to my mother and father. I am thrilled that that ordeal is over. I love my mother and worry so much about her, and I just want her to know that I am okay and am there every day. I am there anytime you talk to me. Always. I like the yellow flowers. There's no way I can fix what has happened, and I had to realize I did not cause the situation. I felt responsible for all the horrible things going on with my family because it was about me, and it didn't help that I died a bad death. But it's all right now; I'm with family and continue to grow. There are some horses nearby, and I do go to see them. I understand my living life is over, but my spiritual life is continuing. It is not the end; this is not goodbye. Please pretend I went on vacation to a wonderful beach where it's always summer. You'll never be without me ever again. Please, please live. I must go now, but don't worry it is all beautiful."

Thus, finishes the communication I had with Olga, a beautiful bright, lovely spirit. After the connection, I felt lighter. I had experienced such upset at reading her story I did not know what to expect. The communication was 200% different than what I was anticipating. Olga is a young lady now. Spirits are not babies; the physical self may be young, but the soul is much older, already developed energy. Those who pass as infants and children grow in spirit, and once they are situated, then they evolve. To me, it was surprising how little Olga allowed the situation with Anatoly Moskvin to affect her adversely. She's now free in the spirit world where she belongs.

Carl Tanzler - the man from whom I feel Anatoly Moskvin was reincarnated

Carl Tanzler (German: Feb. 8, 1877-July 3, 1952) born as Karl or Georg Karl in Dresden, Germany is sometimes referred to as Count Carl von Cosel, a microbiologist and bacteriologist in Key West, Florida who developed an obsession with a young tuberculosis patient, Maria Elena "Helen" Milagro de Hoyos (July 31, 1909-Oct. 25, 1931) that continued after her death. He removed the body from its tomb and lived with her corpse for seven years until Hoyos' sister called the authorities on the situation.

Tanzler emigrated to the United States in 1926, settling in Zephyrhills, Florida, where his sister already lived, and his wife and two daughters later joined him. The next year he left his family and took a job at the U.S. Marine Hospital in Key West, Florida under the name Carl von Cosel.

During his childhood in Germany, and later while traveling briefly in Italy, Tanzler claimed to have been visited by his dead ancestor, Countess Anna Constantia von Cosel, who revealed the face of his true love, an exotic dark-haired woman, to him. He met this beauty on April 22, 1930, while working in Key West. Maria Elena "Helen" Milagro de Hoyos, a local Cuban-American woman, was brought to the hospital by her mother to be examined. Tanzler immediately recognized her from his earlier 'visions.'

Elena and her two sisters were daughters of a local cigar maker and his wife. She married a man that soon left her after she miscarried the couple's only child, and she was never divorced. Eventually, Elena was diagnosed with tuberculosis and Tanzler attempted to treat her with a variety of medicines and equipment that he brought to her home. Tanzler also showered Hoyos with gifts and reportedly declared his love for her.

Despite Tanzler's best efforts, Hoyos died at her parents' home in 1931. He paid for her funeral and had an above-ground mausoleum built in the Key West Cemetery with the family's permission, which he visited almost nightly. He alleged that when sitting by her grave serenading the corpse with her favorite Spanish song, Elena's spirit would come to him and she would often ask him to take her from the grave. Two years after Elena's burial, Tanzler removed her body from the crypt after dark and carted her on a toy wagon to his home. He wired the bones together, packed the body with rags to keep its form, added glass eyes and dressed her in stockings, jewelry, and gloves. As her skin decomposed, Tanzler replaced it with silk fabric that he had soaked in wax and plaster of Paris. When the hair fell out of her decomposing skull, Tanzler used hair that Hoyos' mother had given to him after the burial to make a wig. Tanzler used perfume, disinfectants, and preserving agents, to mask the odor and slow the decomposition effects of the corpse while he kept the body in his bed.

In October 1940, one of Hoyo's sisters heard rumors that Tanzler was sleeping with the disinterred body of Elena and confronted him at his home. Tanzler revealed Elena was laying in his bed and told the sister "you may visit anytime you wish." The authorities were immediately notified, and Tanzler was arrested for 'wantonly and maliciously destroying a grave and removing a body without authorization.' After a psychiatric examination found him mentally competent to stand trial, the case was dropped because the statute of limitations for the crime had expired. Tanzler was released.

Hoyos's body was examined by physicians and pathologists and put on public display at the Dean-Lopez Funeral Home, where it was viewed by over 6000 people due to nationwide sensation created by newspapers. The public generally sympathized with Tanzler and regarded him as an eccentric "romantic." Hoyos's body was eventually returned to the Key West Cemetery where her remains were placed in a secret, unmarked grave to prevent further interference.

Although it was not reported at the time of autopsy, research has revealed (most notably by authors Harrison and Swicegood) evidence of necrophilia with Hoyos's corpse. In 1972, over thirty years after the autopsy and case dismissal, two attendees (Dr. DePoo and Dr. Foraker) recalled that a paper tube had been inserted in the vaginal area of the corpse allowing for intercourse. With no existing photographs from the autopsy or public display showing a tube, some believe that the necrophilia allegation is questionable.

Tanzler wrote an autobiography in 1947 that appeared in the Pulp publication, *Fantastic Adventures* and he was granted United States citizenship in 1950. He had moved near his wife who apparently helped support him in his later years. Although Tanzler was separated from his obsession, he used a death mask to create a life-sized model of Hoyos and lived with it until he died in 1952. His body was not found for three weeks. His obituary mentioned a waxen image wrapped in silk sitting on a shelf in a metal cylinder; and although the article stated that his body was discovered on the floor behind one of his organs, some say Tanzler was in the arms of the

Hoyos effigy. Further, it has been written (most notably by Swicegood) that Tanzler either switched the bodies or that Hoyos's remains were secretly returned to him, and that he died with the real corpse of Hoyos.

Elena Hoyos Psychic Conversation

The next spirit I did try to contact was Elena Hoyas who had been the obsession of Carl Tanzler. Her transition happened in the 1930s, so she has moved on which can be considered reincarnation or something else, but she is definitely moved further into the universal brain. By accessing energy there, I have been given what I would consider a phone message. Her comments on Carl Tanzler was that she was sympathetic to his plight and understands it, but it was not to her liking. She thought he was a very pathetic individual and considered him an oddball. She did not, in life, respond to his obsession and her last comment to me about Carl was to call him 'dirty old man,' with which her sisters agree. That was where the communication stopped. These two first communications (Olga and Elena) were different than what I expected, so I hope you find interest in these outcomes. It shows each spirit has a personality of its own just like us because they are us. Now onto the next parting of the veil...

Frozen Charlotte

In America from the 1840s through the 1920s or at least around World War I there was a very peculiar doll sold by the millions that was actually based upon a corpse. Each doll was known as Frozen Charlotte, and her male companion was called Frozen Charlie. My maternal grandmother had hundreds of these when she was a little girl in the 1890s. Hardware stores would sell the dolls in large barrels, and they ranged in size from about 1 to 18 inches. The smallest ones were called Penny Dolls because they cost one cent and each barrel held hundreds of them.

You may be wondering how a doll based on a corpse would be something with which parents would allow their children to play. According to Wikipedia the name of the doll comes from a folk ballad called *Fair Charlotte* by William Lorenzo Carter that, in turn, was based on a poem *A Corpse Going To A Ball* by Seba Smith. These were supposedly based upon a true story from the 1840s of a girl who was too vain to wrap up warmly while riding with her beau through the snow in an open carriage during the dead of winter. By the time they reached the ball, she was frozen stiff. Following is one version of the ballad, but of course, there are others.

FAIR CHARLOTTE

Now, Charlotte lived on the mountainside,
In a bleak and dreary spot;
There was no house for miles around,
Except her father's cot.

And yet on many a wintry night,
Young swains were gathered there;
For her father kept a social board,
And she was very fair.

One New Year's Eve as the sun went down,
Far looked her wishful eye
Out from the frosty window pane
As merry sleighs went by.

In a village fifteen miles away,
Was to be a ball that night;
And though the air was heavy and cold,
Her heart was warm and light.

How brightly beamed her laughing eye,
As a well-known voice was heard;
And driving up to the cottage door,

Her lover's sleigh appeared.

*"O, daughter dear," her mother cried,
"This blanket 'round you fold;
It is a dreadful night tonight,
You'll catch your death of cold."*

*"O, nay! O, nay!" young Charlotte cried,
And she laughed like a gypsy queen;
"To ride in blankets muffled up,
I never would be seen.*

*"My silken cloak is quite enough,
You know 'tis lined throughout;
Besides I have my silken scarf,
To twine my neck about."*

*Her bonnet and her gloves were on,
She stepped into the sleigh;
Rode swiftly down the mountain side,
And o'er the hills away.*

*With muffled face and silent lips,
Five miles at length were passed;
When Charles with few and shivering words,
The silence broke at last.*

*"Such a dreadful night I never saw,
The reins I scarce can hold."
Fair Charlotte shivering faintly said,
"I am exceeding cold."*

*He cracked his whip, he urged his steed
Much faster than before;
And thus, five other dreary miles
In silence were passed o'er.*

*Said Charles, "How fast the shivering ice
Is gathering on my brow."
And Charlotte still more faintly said,
"I'm growing warmer now."*

*So, on they rode through frosty air
And glittering cold starlight,
Until at last the village lamps
And the ballroom came in sight.*

They reached the door and Charles sprang out,
He reached his hand for her;
She sat there like a monument,
That has no power to stir.

He called her once, he called her twice,
She answered not a word;
He asked her for her hand again,
And still she never stirred.

He took her hand in his - O, God!
'Twas cold and hard as stone;
He tore the mantle from her face,
Cold stars upon it shone.

Then quickly to the glowing hall,
Her lifeless form he bore;
Fair Charlotte's eyes were closed in death,
Her voice was heard no more.

And there he sat down by her side,
While bitter tears did flow;
And cried, "My own, my charming bride,
You never more will know."

He twined his arms around her neck,
He kissed her marble brow;
His thoughts flew back to where she said,
"I'm growing warmer now."

He carried her back to the sleigh,
And with her he rode home;
And when he reached the cottage door,
O, how her parents mourned.

Her parents mourned for many a year,
And Charles wept in the gloom;
Till at last her lover died of grief,
And they both lie in one tomb.

Just imagine: The Frozen Charlotte doll was the *Barbie Doll* of the era and many children played with them. The smaller ones were also used as charms and even put into cakes as party favors. There is even a Frozen Charlotte dessert recipe made with ladyfingers and sorbet or ice cream that is available on several sites, but I doubt many know the history of the dessert's namesake. The dolls themselves were usually pale white with black hair, or occasionally blonde. Most of the dolls were nude, but a few had molded clothing on them. The bigger ones were sometimes glazed on the front and unglazed on the back so that they could float in the bathtub much like a rubber ducky.

I asked both of my grandmothers about their childhood dolls because they were Victorians, and these were the type toys with which they would play. My maternal grandmother 'Granny' of course told me she had hundreds of the little white Penny dolls. She also had many China dolls with white skin and black hair, and she kept them all in a trunk. In 1902 when she was six, her father died, but the last thing he gave her was a bisque doll with a parasol. After her father's death, she and her mother had to live with her aunts who tended to be rather mean. Later, when she was a teenager my grandmother had to go away for a week; her aunts gave all of her dolls to neighbors including the doll from her father which was one of the few things she had left of him. She was forever scarred emotionally by her aunts' cruelty. She loved her dolls, but she eventually had 12 children who became her living dolls.

My paternal grandmother who we called 'Grandma' told me she was given a China doll with white skin and black hair when she was about 10, which was based on the Frozen Charlotte except this one had a cloth body. She remembered she had left it on the bed one day while her mother was making the bed. When the sheets were flipped, Grandma's China doll was smashed into pieces against the footboard of the bed, and since they were poor, she never had another doll.

Just about every little Victorian girl had one of these dolls. The corpse Charlotte and her boyfriend who grieves himself to death remain companions even in the world of playthings. China dolls and Frozen Charlottes can be found by the ton online. If you're looking for those particular ones based upon the girl in the ballad, make sure to get one with china white skin. In Germany where most of these originated, the factories would bury the rejects. Now, a hundred years later, one can pay to go there to dig up broken doll heads by the shovelful. Some of these broken pieces can also be found online, ready for repair or to display as is. I have several beautiful heads and faces that are quite rare which I would never be otherwise able to own. Some of them have snoods and are molded with feathers in their headdresses. It's a fascinating part of history and our need for morbid playthings. It reminds me of a 1970s movie whose title says it all: *Children Shouldn't Play with Dead Things.*

Marquis Francesco Longhi

Marquis Francesco Longhi (Italian: 19th Century) born Italian nobility who resided in the Castello Di Fumone of the Lazio region in Italy.

Fumone Castle has a dark history of gruesome events and was used by the Roman Catholic Church for a while as a fortress to torture and house political prisoners. Many people were executed on the property and inside its walls. Unfortunately, even the little Marquis Longhi was murdered; his seven sisters killed him when he was only five years old.

Francesco was the eighth child and beloved son born after seven girls, to Marquise Emilia Caetani Longhi and her husband Marquis Longhi in the early 19th Century. Because he was the only son, he would automatically be the sole heir of the family fortune. All seven sisters would be forced into arranged marriages which they thought unfair and decided the little boy should not inherit anything.

The medical report of the time offers very little information; some say he may have been poisoned, but there is a horrifying rumor of the girls adding tiny shards of glass to his food over several days. The young Marquis began to feel sick, suffering excruciating and unexplained stomach pain. It wasn't long before he started to vomit blood, dying soon after.

Prior to the little Marquis' murder, it had also been reported one of the sisters had stopped an arranged marriage by killing her boyfriend in the same way: tiny pieces of glass added to his meal.

Little Francesco's mother was inconsolable and decided not to bury her son, so she could always see him by her side. He was embalmed, mummified with wax and placed in a crystal box. It is reported that the Marquise was so distraught that she had a painter remove any sign of happiness from all their family portraits. Many said she continued dressing the boy, speaking to him and crying over him until her death.

In the Hall of Archives of the Castle are ancient books and documents as well as an unassuming wooden cabinet. When opened you'll find the transparent display case on top holding the mummified little boy, his face covered by wax, surrounded by his favorite toys and games. The bottom doors open to show the dead child's wardrobe, everything well protected from dust and overly curious tourists.

The castle is said to be haunted, and many visitors have reported hearing the terrible sounds of a woman crying in despair. There have also been accounts of small objects that have been hidden or moved by the spirit of the boy and some claim to have seen small changes of expression on little Marquis Longhi's face.

Marquis Francesco Longhi Psychic Conclusion

This story is one of the saddest in the book: seven sisters concerned the little brother would inherit their parents' money, and they would be forced into arranged marriages, murdered the five-year-old horrifically by feeding him ground up glass. Of course, as you read the mother and father were so distraught over his death that they had him preserved with a wax mask fixed on his face. They placed the body in a glass cabinet and kept him the remainder of their lives. He continues to be on display in the Castello di Fumone (by the way you can rent rooms and stay in the haunted castle). There are stories of the parents that spoke to him, changed his clothes, and played games with the son for whom they could not let go.

I tried to communicate with the spirit of the child, but his spirit transitioned many, many years ago. His mother, on the other hand, can still be heard crying and wandering the rooms. Occasionally, the little boy spirit returns to the property to try and convince his mother to go with him, but she is trapped in a mental state that does not allow her to respond to him as a conscious entity. Eventually, she will be reabsorbed and go through the natural process.

Thinking about this story further, I feel that the sisters probably were not punished in the 1800's since this was a wealthy family with a good name. I have no sympathy for those that murder children. If that had been my child that was killed, and I could not punish the sisters who murdered him cruelly, I would have done things differently. Of course, I'm looking at it from a modern mentality, and sometimes here in the South, we believe some people just need killing. By giving them a false sense of security, I would tell my daughters that we were going to a wonderful event in a nearby city where they could meet all the eligible young men that their hearts desired. I would've made sure they wore their most elegant clothing and packed all their best things. Then taking them in the carriage to the outskirts of a large city, I would put money in each of their bags and set them on the street informing them they were no longer my daughters, or any worth to me. They were now on their own, and since they didn't want arranged marriages, they should find a way to live. I would suggest they make it all work for them. They could never come home again for I would install new guard dogs. Then I would get in my carriage and leave them standing in the street. You may think it's a little harsh, but it's my fantasy response to killer sisters.

La Pascualita

I remember the first time I learned about La Pascualita was sometime in the late 1980s; long before anything ever "trended" on the internet, and yes, there was a time before the internet. The story was on some televised show about mysterious items, and I didn't hear about it again until just a few years ago.

In 1929 in Chihuahua Mexico, according to legend, a young girl died from a black widow bite just before her wedding. The heartbroken girl's mother, Pascuala Esparza, owned a dress shop, wherein 1930 there appeared in the window a manikin dressed in a bridal gown that had an amazing resemblance to her deceased daughter. Not only did the face look like her, but the hands were incredibly detailed with lifelines and wrinkles just like a real hand. Many people believed she was actually the well-preserved corpse of the shop owner's daughter, not just a facsimile. Tales began circulating of the manikin's eyes following shoppers' movements around the store. Stories were also told that the body would move, and the hands would change position. According to more folklore, a lovestruck French magician appears at night, bringing the corpse to life to take her out so she can enjoy the area's nightlife. These stories have been ongoing for 88 years.

In my assessment, the first thing I have to say is that we today do not have a process that can preserve a corpse perfectly over a week or two, much less for 88 years. Secondly, there's no way this is an actual corpse that has been exposed to light, air, temperature, and microscopic organisms because it looks too good; however, because of the realistic face which matches the daughter's image, I tend to think this may be a postmortem casting of the daughter much like a death mask. La Pascualita is very possibly a postmortem doll. The relic may have spiritual energy infused into the vessel - not to mention 88 years of energy and attention focused on her, and it is very possible this figure has a consciousness. It is beyond belief how incredibly realistic La Pascualita's hands appear, and the difference between her ultra-realistic face compared to other manikins and storefront dummies from the 1920s era is very distinguishable.

Shop workers who have to change the dresses become very nervous around the figure. La Pascualita is an extraordinary and wondrous creation that I would love very much to go see in person, and since she has worn wedding dresses for the last eight decades, I would say to her "never the bride's maid always the bride."

Grave Robbing and the Wax Anatomical Doll

Grave robbing has been a shocking practice known since the time of the Egyptian pharaohs, and for about two centuries China has maintained the morbid activity. Europe began suffering from the problem at least from the 1500s while the United States has dealt with it since the colonies' early days. In certain areas continued desecrations were seriously problematic through the 20th century. In the beginning, grave robbing was done mostly to steal anything of value including jewelry, gold teeth, and even clothing, but when medical colleges began teaching anatomy, there was a shortage of available bodies. Occasionally remains of prisoners executed or any unclaimed bodies from orphanages, insane asylums or prisons were allowed to be used as practice pieces. Unfortunately for the up-and-coming doctors, there still weren't enough bodies available to meet the demand. Incredibly, medical schools began paying grave robbers to search graveyards and find the freshly buried to supply the anatomical needs of the laboratory classes. These thieves became known as *the resurrectionists*.

Grave robbing became somewhat of an epidemic. It was such a severe situation that special coffins were created to prevent body snatching. Iron cages were made to go over the graves for protection, and some bodies wore collars around the neck that were bolted to the bottom of each casket. Concrete vaults were built, and large stones were placed over the grave to prevent theft, but even these precautions were ineffective to the persistent thieves. Since the body itself became the item of worth, special houses were created for storage; there, the cadavers were allowed to rot for 30 days to make them too unappealing to be stolen.

There are some stories up until modern times about grave robbing famous bodies, including Charlie Chaplin and Abraham Lincoln. One failed attempt was to steal President Lincoln from his grave which then led to a very complicated moving and hiding of his body for over 20 years. In 2015, Livius Drusus wrote about a particularly horrifying story of John Scott Harrison, the Representative from Ohio who died May 25, 1878, and was then buried four days later. During Harrison's funeral, someone noticed that a nearby grave that of Augustus Devin who had died of tuberculosis and was buried the previous week had been robbed. Harrison's sons Benjamin, John, and Carter saw to it that their father's brick vault was reinforced with three large stone slabs, and had concrete poured on top to deter grave robbers. They also paid a watchman $30 to guard their father's grave for 30 days to make sure the body was beyond usability. The next day John and his cousin George Eaton obtained a search warrant and with three Cincinnati policemen went to look for the body of Devin at the Medical College of Ohio. In their search and to their utter shock instead of Augustus Devin they found Representative Harrison's nude body hanging from a noose awaiting its time on the dissection table. Devin was found in a vat of brine (similar to embalming fluid) to preserve the body until it was needed.

Although the janitor was arrested for body snatching, the college posted his $5000 bail and stood behind his decision to buy bodies. Harrison's sons sued the college, but unfortunately, no record exists of the civil suit's outcome because the results were destroyed in a fire that burned down the courthouse.

Wax model making was usually a male-dominated endeavor, but one French female, Marie Grosholtz Tussaud (1761 - 1850) taught by Dr. Philippe Curtis, became the art teacher of King Louis XVI's sister, Madame Elizabeth, and was allowed to live in the court of Versailles. Later, she became known for making postmortem castings of famous people killed by the guillotine; she even made a cast of Marie Antoinette's decapitated head as well as Louis XVI and her friend Madame Elizabeth. She almost lost her own head until an intervention by Curtis saved her. Instead of losing her head, she made copies of those who did. Her career and waxworks are still known today in Madame Tussauds Wax Museum in many cities around the world.

Anna Mazzola wrote an interesting story, *The Woman Who Created Corpses: Mademoiselle Bihéron and Her Anatomical Dolls*, which is about Marie Marguerite, born in 1719, the daughter of an apothecary. She rose to fame in Paris as a self-trained maker of wax anatomical models, a practical solution to the body shortage for experimentation in 18th-Century medical classes. Bihéron would attend hospital and graveyard corpses to make plaster castings to produce detailed wax copies of the dissected bodies created from beeswax and her secret ingredients. She would then paint them or use thread to imitate the details of the removable body parts, membranes and cutaway sections that highlighted different body systems. Each model would have taken months to complete and would be very expensive. Her work was explicit, and she exhibited her unique art collection in a cabinet in her home. To the Académie Royale des Sciences, Bihéron demonstrated a model of a pregnant woman complete with removable parts and fetuses. Word spread quickly of her work which attracted a broad audience including surgeons, academicians, scientists, and artists. In the early 1770s, Bihéron exhibited her models in London.

Jakob Jonas Björnståhl wrote to Carl Linnaeus that: 'Bihéron makes models of parts of the body that are absolutely lifelike. And they do not break. She does not reveal what material they are made of, although it seems as if they were made of wax mixed with something.'

I have done work with wax, and it is a very difficult substance with which to work. Wax looks to be very fragile but indeed can be very sturdy, and if Bihéron used resins with her wax, it could have been like an early version of plastic. Copies may have been beautiful and a fantastic idea but inevitably that would've required a costly piece of equipment so apparently and unfortunately it did not catch on. If you're able to find examples of her work, they are beautiful. Instead of using explicitly created anatomical models colleges chose to continue the art of grave robbing and dissecting stolen corpses. They gave new meaning to the phrase getting your hands dirty.

Robert the Doll

I remember hearing about *Robert the Doll* in the mid-to-late 1980s, and of course, it caught my attention, because who doesn't love a possessed doll story? I barely remembered the figure was owned by an artist who lived in Key West, and upon research, I found out his name: Robert Eugene Otto. He was from a very prominent family in that area and was very eccentric.

Following are two stories of this doll's possible creation: the first one involves a nanny or a young voodoo priestess who made a replica of Otto, wearing a sailor suit just like he had dressed as a child around 1904. He took the doll with him everywhere, and it was his only friend. The second story suggests Otto's mother purchased the doll as a birthday gift while on vacation in Germany. The figure was made by the famous Steiff Company who produced beautiful teddy bears.

Otto left the doll in Key West while studying art in Europe. When he married Annette Parker in 1930, they returned to Florida to live in the family home until their deaths: Robert Otto died in 1974, and his wife, two years later. The house including the doll was sold to Myrtle Reuter who owned it until the 1990s when it was again sold to someone who now operates a B&B or guest house.

Because the doll is believed to have supernatural abilities, it was given to the East Martello Museum in Key West, Florida in 1994 where it rose to international attention and became a tourist attraction. Just like a child, this doll can move around and can change its facial expressions. It can also be heard giggling and talking. It is widely believed that this doll has a consciousness and is aware of those around him.

Young Otto was inseparable from this doll and would blame mishaps and unusual occurrences upon the toy, which also apparently had the knack of being able to disappear for periods of time. Of course, there are many people who, out of fear, have associated unfortunate life experiences and happenings after viewing the doll in the museum. There are claims of accidents, legal problems, failed marriages, anything that could possibly go wrong, blamed upon this doll.

I long for the day that I visit *Robert the Doll* and look at him in close proximity. I saw a couple of years ago a famous ghost hunter was given the opportunity to hold the toy, and he intimidated the doll on purpose to get a reaction. I feel that is an inappropriate way to deal with any metaphysical being that may be living inside that vessel.

Looking at it as a psychic, I do believe there is something to this entity. Of course, as I've said before, dolls are actually versions of us, and it is very easy to ingrain or to inject consciousness into these inanimate objects. When I look at *Robert the Doll*, I have a sense of loneliness because it misses its original owner; and because it is a consciousness ingrained in the doll and not exactly a spirit, it cannot pass on to rejoin its *master* in the afterlife. And yes, I do believe it gets aggravated by taunts from onlookers or strangers who do not take into consideration that this may be an entity with feelings and emotions.

In a way, I also believe this doll has a voodoo vibe which would mean to me it needs to be dealt with carefully; the initial essence has weakened, but it is still conscious. At one point in the doll's existence it was treated basically like a brother by Otto who took it everywhere he went, treating and loving it just like it was another human being; so, it has a sense of sadness, and I would very much like to *converse* with this amazing vessel.

I advise others to be very careful about provoking this being because if it is of a voodoo nature, it would be able to strike out in retaliation. I don't believe it is purposely hurting people randomly, but I do think when people mistreat him, he may lash out in a child-like fashion if his feelings are hurt, and one may get *it* in return. So, approach *Robert* with caution, possibly apprehension; do not antagonize him, for if you do and something bad happens, it's not his fault but your own. Proceed with kindness and respect, and possibly you will get to see something very rare - a glimpse of magic in the form of a doll named *Robert*.

Shabti Doll

Shabti Dolls according to an article by Joshua J Mark in 2012 were funerary figures used in ancient Egypt to help the dearly departed as workers or slaves in the afterlife. If my memory serves me, there were other beliefs where it was customary to kill and bury workers or slaves to assist the wealthy deceased individual, but in Egypt, in my opinion, they realized it was a waste to kill healthy workers to assist the dead beyond the grave. At first, the figures were created to represent the deceased themselves, but then by the time of the New Kingdom (1570-1069 BCE), these figures were designed to portray anonymous workers to fulfill the needs of the deceased in the spiritual realm. Each doll was inscribed with a spell to specify the particular function of that figure. There is a very famous list named the *Coffin Texts* which dates from 2143-2040 BCE, and the most famous is Spell 472 which involves getting the shabti to work for their owner in the hereafter.

Egyptians viewed the afterlife as a mirror image of life itself, requiring extras (Shabti) to assist in reaching an individual's work goal. It is believed the God of the Dead, Osiris, was in charge of public works and the purpose of the Shabti was to answer for the deceased when called upon to work. *The Book of the Dead* contains spells to be spoken by the soul at different times for different purposes in the afterlife. It didn't matter if you were rich or poor you could have the help of these spiritual workers for eternity; there were paupers as well as kings buried with these figures. Of course, the quality and number of the dolls can tell a lot about who the deceased was as well as their status in life. Shabtis are another example that many dolls were not created to be playthings but instead vessels to harbor energy spirits and spells - not exactly your typical Barbie off the shelf!

L'Inconnue de la Seine and the CPR Doll

When I was a young man of about 16 years old in the late 1970's, part of gym class at school was learning cardiopulmonary resuscitation (CPR). My teacher (Mr. Coppenger) a typical jock was thoroughly disgusted by me, a frail artist. I had trouble with this man until one day during CPR certification. He instructed us to "shake the dummy and ask, 'are you, all right?' before sticking your tongue down its throat." Please understand, all this CPR stuff kind of grossed me out, but I was determined to pass the test and get my certificate. It helped that I thought my teacher was an ass and wanted me to fail - believe me, he tried.

The rubber or vinyl dummies we used had to be wiped down with alcohol before you put your mouth on them. When it came to my turn to show my skills, I took the green alcohol wipe and sanitized the female dummy's mouth; then, in a very dramatic and comical way, I hauled off and slapped the dummy's face yelling "are you dead?!" Before I knew it, the teacher and my classmates were rolling on the floor screaming in laughter, and from that moment on the ice was broken. The teacher thought I was a hoot and didn't give me another ounce of trouble.

In the 1980's, I learned that the rubber female dummy face I had to kiss in CPR class was based on a death mask from the 1800's. At first, it grossed me out, and then I felt guilty for slapping her poor little face. At the time I was somewhat fascinated to uncover that bit of information, but I actually forgot about it until putting this book together. Following is the history of *L'Inconnue de la Seine* (English: The Unknown Woman of the Seine):

L'Inconnue de la Seine was an unidentified young woman whose body was pulled out of the Seine River at the Quai du Louvre in Paris around the late 1880s. Her body showed no signs of violence or foul play, and suicide was suspected. She was believed to be around 16 years of age, but the identity of the beautiful girl was never discovered. No one came forward to claim her, and no one was looking for her which should have been the unfortunate ending of a tragic story, but it doesn't end there.

A pathologist was so taken by the sleeping beauty quality of her expression that he decided to preserve it. Using a technique prevalent in the world of antiquity, he made a death mask or a copy of her face in plaster. The practice to purchase copies of famous people's death masks such as those of Abraham Lincoln, Napoleon, and famous actors became widespread.

In the late 1800's - early 1900's, thousands of copies of *L'Inconnue de la Seine* were produced and became a feature on the walls of many artists' homes and studios. She was compared to the *Mona Lisa* because of her secret smile; many had a morbid curiosity of why she died with such a beautiful smile on her lips.

This girl more than likely was a destitute person in unfortunate circumstances who cannot have possibly imagined that for centuries she would become an ideal of beauty. Her face hung in homes of the poor as well as those of the wealthy. She has inspired numerous works in literature, photography, and art. Actresses for many years based their beauty upon her face; from the advent of film, several silent screen stars up to celebrities in the 1950's appeared to have copied the look of the *L'Inconnue de la Seine.*

In 1958 as fate would have it, the original first aid mannequin was created by Peter Safar and Asmund Laerdal, and they needed a face to launch this new tool, so that of the *L'Inconnue de la Seine* was chosen. The CPR dummy was called *Resusci Anne* and was used in numerous CPR courses beginning in 1960. She is also known as *Rescue Anne* and *CPR Annie*. *L'Inconnue de la Seine* has become known as one of the most kissed faces of all time, and in an ironic twist of fate, the girl believed to have killed herself has now become the tool which teaches others to save lives. Now that really gives her something to smile about.

Voodoo Doll

In any wicked book about dolls, we have to include the voodoo doll. Most of us are familiar with the image of a voodoo doll stuck with pins, and have even seen television shows, movies, or read stories related to zombies. Many of us have also heard strange tales of New Orleans' mysterious and beautiful Voodoo priestess Marie Laveau. These are the stuff of legends but there are usually grains of truth in those legends, and I am here to explore some of those with you.

You can't truly appreciate the voodoo doll without exploring the history of the Voodoo religion or touching on slavery which is what ultimately brought the practice of Voodoo to the states. Although the exact origins of Voodoo remain unknown, roots of the practice may have existed even before written word and have beginnings in the Congo region of Africa that later spread to Haiti in the West Indies and then beyond.

Slavery, known as human trafficking today, is something very primitive in human nature that unfortunately still exists in the world. As of now according to Wikipedia, there are 21 million to 46 million people around the world that are enslaved; this includes traditional (or *chattel* (chattel, meaning personal property) slavery, child labor, and sex slavery which are all terrible blights as is the slavery of old. In the Dark Ages of the 1500s, African slave trade was introduced to Europe; and later, in the 17th and 18th centuries, it expanded to the Americas. During this time the people being taken from their homes brought with them their religious beliefs, and upon arrival in the thirteen colonies, it was a rule to convert them to Christianity within a week, banishing their spiritual leanings. Due to the harsh circumstances, many slaves continued their spirituality quietly and used it as a way to survive.

In our modern sensibilities looking back at slavery it's easy for us to say, "oh I would have done this, or I would have done that," but in reality, you have to realize that is bullshit. You could not defend yourself, speak your mind, or even make eye contact, at least not in the majority of situations. Owned like cattle, you, your wife and your children could be sold and even killed. Of course, some owners treated their slaves as family and maybe also became beloved. Many white children were cared for or raised by slaves, and many became closer to the slaves than they were their parents. Some people were against slavery, and they would be punished or killed when they tried to stop the evil slave machine. The Underground Railroad was born to assist in freeing slaves by any means possible, but still many were stuck in horrible conditions. Voodoo practitioners turned to the spirits to have them help in punishing evildoers and protecting their people. Some magic was used to heal, some to hurt, or to kill. Between 1791 and 1804 in Haiti empowered by Voodoo, the slaves revolted and eventually they were able to dislodge the French colonists who left the country running for their lives.

Some of these colonists migrated to Louisiana taking with them some of their French-speaking slaves bringing Voodoo to New Orleans. The practice was never able to grow as strong as it was in Haiti, and although it was beaten down quite a few times, Voodoo stayed and survived.

Voodoo began as a positive system with a central character named *Bondye*, a good god who was a creator but removed from human affairs and direct contact with them. The word *voodoo* means spirit, and practitioners believe in particular spirits, *Loas (also ioas or Iwas)*, who could help them to meet any need. In ritual, it is common for a Loa to possess a follower, speaking to the voodoo community. Starting out as a very positive religion, Voodoo did take on darker undertones.

In the 19th century, the mysterious priestess Marie Laveau became the Voodoo Queen of New Orleans, and I believe she is one of the most important aspects of this history. After the Civil War when slavery was abolished, the recently freed black people had to figure out how to be financially independent, and there weren't a lot of options in poverty. Voodoo practitioners discovered they could earn money by using their belief system: charms, spells, candles, and voodoo dolls became a way to reach economic freedom. Those people who were good at their art collected clientele who were searching for ways to magically achieve their goals. The seller of the charm would also put spells upon the buyer to gain repeat business, but for other customers, they would return out of fear of not enriching the *Boka*. Boka is a term I learned somewhere long ago that may be colloquial, referring to a practicing priest. Marie Laveau was at the top of her game, and every rich man in New Orleans that needed magic came to her. Even now her store and tomb are legendary and a part of the cultural history and tourism business of New Orleans.

Forms of Voodoo still exist around the world including areas of Africa, as well as in Haiti, Brazil, and the United States. There are positive practitioners and dark practitioners. One of the tools in the arsenal of the dark voodoo practitioner is the voodoo doll. The doll is a likeness of the human form. To use this tool, elements of the target/victim are woven into the effigy itself: hair, nail clippings, jewelry, clothing - anything that has the energy or the DNA of the target. The likeness is charged up in ritual. The spell which is an energy sphere of information concerning the recipient also includes what the priest or priestess expects to happen once the magic reaches that target. The energy sphere is magnetized to the energy of the victim using that target's DNA, and when it is released, it follows the energy trail to the designated person, downloads into their system, and the spell begins. It can be very intense and frightening if the practitioner is skilled enough in energy work. I have seen several instances of Voodoo in the aftermath.

As a young man of 18 I became a Wiccan, and then I became a third-degree Gardenarian. In my studies, I also looked at other beliefs such as Buddhism, Voodoo, and Santeria. Know that there is a difference between Voodoo and Santeria, but it is beyond the scope of this book. I have encountered several Santeria priests and priestesses through friends, as well as several witches I know who take elements of Voodoo and Santeria and use those in their magical practices. The Voodoo priests I have met are afraid of witches which is very funny to me.

Now for this book, I will relate a story I have never told. As a psychic, I have visions and vivid dreams which can be very prophetic. 25 years ago, I was given a voodoo doll as a gag gift from a tourist shop in New Orleans. It was a very nicely made piece, and it was my first experience with voodoo dolls. About ten years ago I had a dream that turned out to be a definite prophetic warning:

I dreamed of a magic circle with a life-size antique style coffin - wide at the top, skinny at the bottom, and covered in shiny black lacquer. I'm standing outside of the circle with my friend that I have taken care of for fifteen years, Judith (she was mystical, but because of her disabilities she was vulnerable). In the dream, she's to my left, and we are standing outside of the circle in this black room watching the coffin. The lid opens on its own, and inside it's lined with white satin. Lying in this box is a young man with a mustache and goatee that seems familiar. Then on its own, the lid slams shut, and the coffin begins to shake violently. All of a sudden it opens and a life-size voodoo doll, it's body made of burlap, appears in the coffin. It gets out and with a very sinister smile on its face begins walking in a strange gait towards Judith. It continues to walk through the circle and grabs my friend's arm and starts dragging her towards the coffin. I know it is going to put her in the coffin which means death. I immediately step forward separating her from the voodoo doll, and when I do, it goes back to the coffin gets inside and closes the lid.

Immediately when I woke up, I knew it was some warning for me not to interfere for some reason. I called a witch friend of mine to relate the dream, and she knew exactly about what I was speaking. The previous week a terrible event had happened: a group of witches and metaphysical people, several I knew and all who definitely knew better, were bored and began doing something that, in my opinion, is very stupid and extremely dangerous; even though they are not Voodoo practitioners, for fun, they started performing circles and calling Loas into people there and enjoyed watching the possessions - they thought it was a great hoot. One particular young man, a sweet, kind, gentle person, was invited that my friend and I both knew; he also happened to have a mustache and goatee (the man I saw in my dream). He and his wife went to the circle thinking it was sweat lodge experience (a spiritually grounding ceremony involving meditation that may last several hours). Without telling him, the group called the spirits, and it just so happened a Loa entered this young man, and they got a blast out of him being possessed. Afterward, everyone went home. Unfortunately, Loas can kill a practitioner if displeased.

That night after arriving back with his wife, the usually gentle young man suddenly became possessed again and tried to strangle his wife. He then suffered a fatal heart attack. All of this happened because a group of people was 'playing.' The voodoo doll dream was a warning not to get involved, and I did not. I do not know at this time whatever happened to the rest, but at some point, I have a feeling their lives did not go well.

During my ghost walk in Tennessee called *Chattanooga Chills Ghost Tour* (currently on hiatus until filmed for pay per view) there are no less than six stories told resulting directly from Voodoo. Several priest and priestesses in 1880 were respected and feared in Chattanooga. One lady, Old Aunt Lou, was famous for her charms and it is said that if she stomped her walking staff on the ground, she could travel through time. Then there was one Boka known for taking his cane drawing a line in the dirt street if he wanted to put the 'hurt' on someone. This, of course, was in the days before cars and everyone walked. He drew the line where he knew his victim would cross, and once they stepped over the line, the spell would be cast upon them.

There are several tales during 1880s newspapers of stones raining down onto houses of targeted people while sometimes two to three hundred people watched. This was a tool of intimidation used by skilled Voodoo practitioners. The papers reported one case where the local rednecks were shooting at the falling rocks that were dropping from a great distance ranging in size from pebbles to 5-pound stones. After the 1880s the phenomena stopped, and I believe either the practitioners died or became unable to unleash their skills further.

Almost every city has stories following the War Between the States. Actually, I admire that people who have been so opposed and put upon, found a way to give a comeuppance. I have seen the aftermath of Voodoo and the use of dolls several times, and I have to say whether you believe it or not it is a very powerful element. There are many things in this world that we cannot see, but just because you cannot see it does not mean it does not exist. Hopefully, this has been a cautionary tale not to play with the embers of an ancient fire unless you are prepared to be burned.

Luk Thep Doll

Thailand is a place of mysterious beliefs, and a few of our stories are connected to that area. From one end of the strange and unusual spectrum to the other, we go from sex dolls to *Luk Thep* dolls. Luk Thep basically means 'child angel' and from what I understand the early ones were created to be the vessels of infant spirits who were lost during miscarriages. A priestess would transfer the spirit into a doll that resembles a real small child or baby, or one similar to the American *Reborn Doll*. It is a very spiritual and individual process that the priestess would tailor the ceremony by choosing the appropriate doll for the purchaser. The concept started off with a priest or priestesses and devoted followers or disciples. Because of the popularity of the dolls now some monks call on a goddess spirit to bless and inhabit the dolls, blessing up to six at a time.

These dolls are so familiar now that certain airlines allow the owner to purchase a seat for the 'child.' The doll is 'fed,' and its clothes are changed as if he or she is a real child. Some people get them because they can't have children of their own; others obtain the dolls believing they will be blessed with money and success. The very rich and famous may have several of these items that sometimes cost into the thousands of dollars. It is believed the better a Luk Thep doll is treated, the more blessings the owner will have in return.

If for any reason the owner becomes disillusioned with the concept, or cannot provide for the doll in the fashion believed deserved, they can return them, but not back to a toy store. In magic, when an inanimate object like a doll has been through a ritual focused on bringing specific - namely spiritual - energy into that container, it then becomes a vessel. At that point, the amount of energy that can be ingrained depends on the energy technician/priest or priestess's skill level.

The critical point I want to make is the idea of embedding anything with what we call *psi* energy which is unseen psychic energy we all have. Psi means the parapsychological psychic phenomena of powers, experiences or events related to the psyche or the mind that can't be explained by established physical laws. If a doll or other vessel is embedded with your psi, it is in essence, inserted with your DNA similar to when a living child is created. The color and type of hair and eyes, facial features, mannerisms, talents, and cellular memory among many other characteristics are all contained within DNA material. Psi energy is an invisible plasma, part of your mystical essence, that exists that can include thought, emotion, and consciousness. It is there even though we cannot see it with our naked eyes. Already the monk, priest or priestess has attempted to fill that vessel with a specific energy or spirit; if you add your particular energy with enough of your psi essence containing your thoughts and emotions, you have just given this energy consciousness.

At that point, the doll or other vessel can feel and may need to feed itself (remember the owners that are 'feeding' their dolls). It is very possible these Luk Thep dolls are basic rudimentary thinking and feeling entities.

If for some reason the owner has to reject the doll, or the doll denies the owner they can be returned or surrendered to a temple, but once something is spiritually created it cannot be destroyed. Of one thing I'm confident, you sure as hell won't be seeing one of these at the toy store next to the barbies and sunshine dolls.

Nagoro, Japan

Nagoro is basically a Japanese ghost town that has been created by people leaving to look for work or by its locals dying off. A little more than a decade ago a resident named Tsukimi Ayano returned to live in her childhood home. She became so lonely that she began to make life-size dolls representing former residents, and she has created about 350 of these effigies to populate the tiny village. Initially, these dolls reminded me of American scarecrows. The first one she made was an image of her father that she placed in the garden performing one of his daily routines. Other figures of now-departed family members have been set around the town to represent them conducting activities they did while alive. The photos of the school are filled with likenesses of children, and stores are filled with customers. There are bikers, fisherman and even elderly couples sitting around doing what they would have done in life. It's all rather eerie and fascinating at the same time - the haunted stares of hundreds of living dolls created to keep Tsukimi company.

Isla de las Munecas (The Island of the Dolls)

Isla de las Munecas (The Island of the Dolls) is a small island south of Mexico City. To this day it is filled with a collection of over a thousand dolls started by the island's caretaker Don Julian Santana Barrera. Legend has it that the caretaker found the corpse of a little girl who had drowned under mysterious circumstances, and he was very disturbed by the experience. Shortly after discovering the victim, Barrera saw a doll floating in the canal that he believed belonged to the young child. As a tribute to the deceased girl, he hung that doll from a tree.

Barrera then began hanging more dolls to appease the girl's spirit who he thought was haunting him and the island. Believing the dolls represent the souls of dead children he began to collect them full time to cover the trees. Barrera continued hanging and displaying dolls for 50 years until his untimely death in 2001. Allegedly, he was found drowned in the same place the young girl had been pulled out of the water so many years before.

Now it is believed that the former caretaker haunts the island along with the children's spirits. Visit the strange place if you're brave enough and see if you can survive the stares from thousands of lifeless dolls on the legendary Isla de las Munecas; hopefully unlike Don Julian Santana Barrera, you will escape the Island of the Dolls.

Ghost Marriages

In China and other parts of Asia, there are ancient rituals, which some believe to be at least 3000 years old, continuing to this day; one of those is ghost marriages of which the origins are mostly unknown. Other forms of these weddings are practiced worldwide, but generally a ghost, or spirit, marriage is a union in which one or both spouses are deceased. These are performed for many reasons including to ensure the family line continues, the marriage of an engaged couple before one member's death, to add an unmarried daughter into a man's family lineage, or to make sure a younger brother is not wed before his elder sibling. The Chinese customs revolve around promoting and preserving the family name and honor, not necessarily caring about an individual's wants or preferences.

The Chinese harbor a distinct bias where males are chosen over females because of the importance of taking care of elderly parents and especially carrying on the family name. From the 1970s until 2016, couples in China were allowed to have one child, and because of the gender preference, if the child was female, it could be aborted or killed just after birth. Because of the laws, there are now over 26 million men and very few women, meaning there are not enough women for the men to marry and there are a lot of men dying as bachelors, known as 'bare branches' because they have no leaves on the family tree.

It is considered a shame upon the family for the son or daughter to die unmarried. The duty of Chinese parents to marry off their children becomes increasingly important for their daughters, since women are only able to acquire membership in descent lines through marriage. Lucky for them there is a local remedy - ghost marriages! Wedding brokers exist to arrange deals between families and find a spouse for the male or female. According to brokers, 30 years ago a corpse bride cost about $1300 American money, but now you can't buy a single bone for under $31,000. It has become a very profitable business.

Chinese households have alters with spirit tablets of the parental ancestors, and a married woman is safely worshiped at the altar of her husband's family. But if an unmarried woman, an 'autumn leaf,' dies the family cannot place her tablet upon the alters to pray for her, she will have no descendants to worship her or make sure that she is part of the family lineage. She will be given a temporary paper tablet that is kept somewhere less honorable. Ghost marriages ensure dead daughters will be safely taken care of in the afterlife through the husband's lineage, ultimately taking the shame away from the girl's family.

An unmarried dying daughter, called an 'autumn leaf,' is thought of as an embarrassment and even a threat to the family and considered mentally challenged for not actively pursuing marriage.

She is not allowed to die in the family home; she will be left to die in an outbuilding, a temple designated for spinsters, or in some cases, just taken outside and allowed to die. This is as much a problem for a man who is not actively pursuing marriage. I knew a gorgeous gay Chinese man who had to get married, and it was terrible because he wasn't allowed to be himself. He had no choice but to get married and have children, which he did, to help take care of his family; that is what is expected, and he did it. In China there is no sense of self, it is for the greater good whatever, the greater good is. If your family expects you to produce, you produce or face the consequences.

A family may refuse to bury a son until a bride is found, scouring the local area for years searching for a family with a dead or dying daughter. It is said when a local female is heard to be in the hospital very sick, dozens of families will rush to the side of the girl's family, and a bidding war begins. The family will sell her while she is still alive, and when she dies, they're delighted because the funeral, in essence, becomes a wedding which will secure a happy afterlife for the child and the rest of the family. Usually, the purchased female will be buried with the corpse-man when she dies.

If a family is wealthy enough, they may be able to tempt a living girl into an arranged ghost marriage allowing them to gain a daughter-in-law, and she is expected to become a caregiver for them permanently. Once the ceremony is final, the family may adopt a child to serve as a grandson, and the adoption contract is placed under the deceased's tablet. Families prefer to select from a brother or other related male who can assign one of his sons to the dead man's lineage. The child himself is entitled to inherit his adoptive deceased father's share of the estate.

In the coal mining sections of China, it is difficult to find a bride for any deceased man. A black market has developed there where females are being murdered and then offered as ghost brides. In 2016, a man named Ma Chonghua from north-west China killed two women with mental disabilities and sold each body for $8,300. The women had come to him to find ghost marriage husbands because they were having a hard time finding spouses; instead, he killed them. Unfortunately, sometimes a girl's family will kill her if she is disabled and sell her for ghost marriages themselves.

In the last few years, several cases of corpse stealing rings have popped up. Men go out and dig up already buried women, brush the bugs off and clean them, falsify death certificates and resell them. The extremely poor may dig up a rotting corpse and use it. There are some that use instead a silver figure or a doll to represent the body. Paper figures can be purchased along with representations of houses, furniture, appliances, clothing, servants and all of the goods that living couples may need when married.

Those are symbolically burned after the marriage ceremony to be used by the couple in the spirit world.

Most of the ghost marriage ceremony is performed following Chinese custom, and the corpse bride is always treated as though she is a living, breathing person. She is fed at the wedding feast, invited into and out of the car, and her arrival at the groom's house is announced. The deceased's tablet is placed inside the effigy to ensure the ghost bride animates the figure and is then placed with the groom's family tablets afterward.

The Chinese are extremely frightened of being haunted by unmarried deceased family members believing they can cause illness, death, and destruction. The family may turn to a medium to speak with the unhappy spirit and set up a ghost marriage to calm the disturbance, right the wrongs, and heal the sick. In *Ghost Marriages Among the Singapore Chinese: A Further Note* by Marjorie Topley, she writes of a 14-year-old Cantonese boy who died then appeared to his mother in a dream a month later saying that he wished to marry a girl who had recently died in Ipoh, Perak. The mother hired a medium who channeled the boy to give the name of the girl, birthplace, age and horoscope details which were found to be compatible with the dead son's horoscope.

There are those who do not wish to involve mediums or any form of divination. Those families believe that the unmarried, dying woman's ghost groom will show himself by picking up a red envelope, usually filled with money, that they place in the middle of the street. When someone picks it up, they rush out from hiding places and announce he is the chosen bridegroom.

If a member of an engaged couple dies before the wedding, the remaining partner may choose to go through with the ceremony with the deceased represented by a symbol of sorts; the groom may be represented by a young, white rooster at the service. Women are hesitant about this form of ghost marriage because it requires the bride/widow to participate in the funeral, adhere to a strict dress code and conduct standards for mourning, take a vow of celibacy, and immediately take up residence with the deceased groom's family. A groom may marry his late fiancée without having to abide by strict mourning rules or remain celibate. There are cases where the living person keeps the photo of the deceased partner for 30 years and then they can get rid of it because it is believed the spirit would have moved on by then.

For those families who have gay sons and daughters, a ghost marriage is a way for them to 'straighten that out.' I don't know about you but I'm a gay person, and I would not want to be married to a stranger to make my family happy - Nope, nope, nope! They just have to figure it out in the afterlife. My final words on this: If a funeral becomes a wedding celebration and if you're ever invited to a ghost marriage bring your incense because it's an excellent place for a Stick Up.

MARK ELLIOTT FILTS

ABOUT THE AUTHOR

Mark Fults is a well-known psychic native to Chattanooga TN now living in Pensacola Fl is the author of 'Chattanooga Chills' in partnership with Teal Gray Worldwide they have created 'Gray Fults Press' to publish their own books ,which already include 'Shades of Angels ' and 'Spirited Tales.'

Mark did illustrations and included several stories in each of Teals bestselling books and has 4 new books of his own forthcoming. 'Corpsewood Catchfly a Witches Tale' available on Amazon, The Psychic Wormstitch.' A psychic tell all book, and 'The Darkest Corner' tales of necrophilia and necromancy, and of course 'Chattanooga Chills Scream Louder' and 'Chattanooga Chills Tales from the Grave.'

As well as several YouTube shows 'Shadows Paranormal 'such as 'Secrets of the Read House' by Stormline Films and working on the song to accompany his upcoming children's book' The Wind is Calling My Name.'

References

Anatoly Moskvin

Kashin, Oleg (3 November 2011). "In Nizhny Novgorod, the scientist-ethnographer made a vault in his apartment". Channel 5, Russia. 6 January 2016.

"In the Nizhny Novgorod region for the man who has committed abuse of dead bodies and burial places are subjected to compulsory medical measures". Investigative Committee of the Russian Federation.

"The investigator told about the high-profile cases". Rossiyskaya Gazeta. 19 January 2012.

"Nekropolistu Anatoly Moskvin extended compulsory treatment". Vesti. 2 August 2015.

Makarova, Albina. "Nizhny Novgorod necrophiliac sentenced to compulsory treatment". Rossiyskaya Gazeta. 14 January 2016.

"Criminal proceedings - CASE number 1-167 / 2012". Leninsky District court of Nizhny Novgorod. 25 May 2012.

"Russian 'grave robber made dolls from girls' corpses'". BBC. 6 March 2012.

Kokin-Slavin, Tatiana (2011). "Detained local historian Anatoly Moskvin-nekropolist". Tanya Tank.

Kokin-Slavin, Tatiana (2011). "Interview with Anatoly Moskvin". Tanya Tank.

"Russian grave digger dresses up 29 bodies and puts them on display at home". The Telegraph. 8 November 2011.

Kashin, Oleg (5 December 2011). "We are confident that it will release". Kommersant.

"Case nekropolista Moskvina postponed until June 26". Criminal Chronicle. 18 June 2015.

"Anatoly Moskvin, the "mummy master", is going to marry". Komsomolskaya Pravda.

"Man, Anatoly Moskvin, Who Mummified Girl's Corpses Dressed Up For Parties 'Not Fit For Trial'". The Huffington Post. 24 October 2014.

Nemtsova, Anna (28 November 2011). "Russian Historian Anatoly Moskvin Collected Dead Girls at Home". The Daily Beast.

"Criminal proceedings - CASE number 1-63 / 2013 (1-469 / 2012;)". Leninsky District court of Nizhny Novgorod. 27 February 2013.

"Nekropolist Anatoly Moskvin continue compulsory treatment".Ru. 9 April 2014.

Wikipedia

Carl Tanzler

Swicegood, Tom (2003). Von Cosel. iUniverse. ISBN 0-595-74652-7.

"A Macabre Love Story". Crime Library. Archived from the original on 2006-08-27. Radiologist Carl von Cosel, 56, became obsessed with one of the tuberculosis patients at the sanitarium where he worked. Her name was Maria Elena de Hoyos and she was a beautiful, 22-year-old woman.

"Rosicrucian Digest". Supreme Council of the Rosicrucian Order. 21 November 2017. – via Google Books.

"The Trial Bay Organ: A Product of Wit and Ingenuity," The Rosicrucian Digest, March 1939, pp.54–58, April 1939, pp.92–96.

Harrison, Ben (2001). Undying Love: The True Story Of A Passion That Defied Death. St. Martin's Press. ISBN 0-312-97802-2. ... Tanzler left Germany, a country that was dispirited and defeated after the First World War, and sailed across the Atlantic Ocean to the United States, ...

Bhikkhu Nyanatusita & Hellmuth Hecker, The Life of Nyanatiloka Thera, Kandy, 2008, pp. 53–54.

Harrison, Ben (2001). Undying Love. St. Martin's True Crime. ISBN 0-312-97802-2.

Sloan, David (1998). Ghosts of Key West. Phantom Press. ISBN 0-9674498-0-4. .

"Autopsy 6: Secrets of the Dead - The Strange Obsession of Dr. Carl Von Cosel". HBO.com. 2005.

Key West Citizen; July 24, 1952

"La Boda Negra: Count Carl von Cosel's macabre obsession with Elena Hoyos -". lynncinnamon.com. Retrieved 21 November 2017.

"The Dollop with Dave Anthony and Gareth Reynolds : 297 - Carl Tanzler". thedollop.libsyn.com.

"Grand Gesture". thisamericanlife.org.

Wikipedia

Frozen Charlotte

"Young Charlotte" - Maine Folklife Center - University of Maine". Maine Folklife Center.

Dolls Antonia Fraser, 1963, p. 62

Coleman. Dorothy S., Elizabeth A. and Evelyn JK.; The Collector's Encyclopaedia of Dolls Volume One, (USA, 1978)

Eaton, Faith; Dolls In Colour (London, 1975)

Melbourne Museum; Frozen Charlotte Doll (Victoria, 2002)

Russell, Nancy (May 3, 2012). "Frozen Charlotte doll a cool find". Columbia Tribune.

Laws, G. Malcolm (1964). Native American Balladry: A Descriptive Study and a Bibliographic Syllabus. Philadelphia: The American Folklore Society. p. 221. ISBN 0-292-73500-6.

Cohen, Norm: Folk Music: A Regional Exploration, p. 24-25 (America, 2005) ISBN 0-313-32872-2

"The Ohio Democrat and Dover advertiser. (Canal Dover, Ohio) 1839-1840, February 28, 1840, Image 1". 1840-02-28. ISSN 2372-7020.

Library of Congress Chroncling American July 9, 2018

Wikipedia

Marquis Francesco Longhi

The Marquis Longhi, killed by his sisters - Emadion

emadion.it/en/mummies/the-marquis-longhi-killed-by-his-sisters

The tragic story of the child mummified Fumone (with video)

www.pilloledistoria

Wikipedia

La Pascualita

La Pascualita – The Mexican Corpse Bride!

www.paranormal-encounters.com/wp/la-pascualita

La Pascualita – Chihuahua, Mexico - Atlas Obscura

www.atlasobscura.com/places/la-pascualita

Wikipedia

Grave Robbing And The Wax Anatomical Doll

The Woman Who Created Corpses: Mademoiselle Bihéron and her Anatomical Dolls – By Anna Mazzola

These Grotesque 18th Century Wax Models Were Made ... - Ranker

www.ranker.com/list/disturbing-1700s-wax-models

Wikipedia

Robert The Doll

'ROBERT THE DOLL". www.robertthedoll.org.

Ella Morton (2013-11-18). "Robert the Haunted Doll: Creeping Out Floridians Since 1904". Slate.com.

"The Story Behind the World's Most Terrifying Haunted Doll". atlasobscura.com. 26 October 2015.

"Artist House - History". Artist House. Artist House, Key West. Retrieved 1 December 2017.

"Robert The Doll – Artist House Key West – Key West Guesthouse". www.artisthousekeywest.com.

"History of Fort East Martello – Key West Art and Historical Society". kwahs.org.

"Fort East Martello Museum (Key West, FL): Top Tips Before You Go (with Photos) – TripAdvisor". www.tripadvisor.com.

"Halloween Story The Legend of Robert the Doll". floridakeystreasures.com. 4 November 2017.

Weikle, Harlan. "TAPS hunts for things that go bump in the night". TBNweekly. Tampa Bay Newspapers.

Shaughnessy, Carol. "Robert the Doll Goes to Vegas". Key Voices. The Florida Keys & Key West. The Monroe County Tourist Development Council.

"The Curse of Robert the Doll (2016)". Rotten Tomatoes. Fandango.

"THE CURSE OF ROBERT THE DOLL". BBFC. British Board of Film Classification.

Wikipedia

Shabati Dolls

Taylor, Richard (2000). 2000. ABC-CLIO. p. 114. ISBN 0-87436-939-8.

Teeter, E (October 1998). "Harry M. Stewart. Egyptian Shabtis". Journal of Near Eastern Studies: 299–300.

ushabti. (2003). In The Macmillan Encyclopedia.

Taylor, Richard. "SHABTI (USHABTI, SHAWABTI)." Death and the Afterlife: a cultural encyclopedia. California: 2000.

Wendy Doniger, Merriam-Webster's Encyclopedia of World Religions, Merriam-Webster 1999, p.1121

Papyrus of Ani; Egyptian Book of the Dead

Coffin Text 472 in A. Gardiner, Egypt of the Pharaohs: An Introduction, p.32

Ian Shaw, The Oxford History of Ancient Egypt, Oxford University Press 2003, p.170

R. N. Longenecker, Life in the Face of Death: The Resurrection Message of the New Testament, Wm. B. Eerdmans Publishing 1998, p.28

"Relics of Ancient Egypt". 1916. The Lotus Magazine. 7 (5): 213-214.

Wikipedia

L'Inconnue De La Seine And The CPR Doll

Chrisafis, Angelique (December 1, 2007). "Ophelia of the Seine". The Guardian Weekend magazine, page 17 – 27. The Guardian.

Elizabeth Bronfen, Over her Dead Body: Death, Femininity and the Aesthetic, MUP, 1992, p. 207

www.bbc.com/news/magazine-24534069

Jeremy Grange (16 October 2013). "Resusci Anne and L'Inconnue: The Mona Lisa of the Seine". BBC News.

"l'Inconnue de la Seine" by Anja Zeidler

Alvarez, Al. The Savage God. A Study of Suicide. New York & London: W.W. Norton & Company, 1971. Page 156.

Sciolino, Elaine (20 July 2017). "At a Family Workshop Near Paris, the 'Drowned Mona Lisa' Lives On". The New York Times.

"A Habit of Dying" by DJ Wiseman

"Der Mouleur, an dem ich jeden Tag vorüberkomme, hat zwei Masken neben seiner Tür ausgehängt. Das Gesicht der jungen Ertränkten, das man in der Morgue abnahm, weil es schön war, weil es lächelte, weil es so täuschend lächelte, als es wüßte."

"... uns jedoch ein zarter Schmetterling, der, sorglos beschwingt, an der Leuchte des Lebens seine feinen Flügel vor der Zeit verflattert und versengt hat."

D. Barton Johnson (1992), "L'inconnue de la Seine" and Nabokov's Naiads, Comparative Literature, 44, 3, p. 225-248.

"Influence and authenticity of l'Inconnue de la Seine". WilliamGaddis.org.

ABT – L'innconue (Accessed 31 May 2015)

CPR Annie, Snopes.com, 21 June 2005. Accessed 3 September 2007

Histories: The girl from the Seine, New Scientist, 23 July 2005

Wikipedia

Voodoo Doll

Armitage, Natalie (2015). "European and African Figural Ritual Magic: The Beginnings of the Voodoo Doll Myth". In Ceri Houlbrook and Natalie Armitage. The Materiality of Magic: An Artifactual Investigation into Ritual Practices and Popular Beliefs.

Faraone, Christopher A. "Binding and Burying the Forces of Evil: The Defensive Use of "Voodoo Dolls" in Ancient Greece". Classical Antiquity.

Hutton, Ronald (1999). The Triumph of the Moon: A History of Modern Pagan Witchcraft. Oxford: Oxford University Press. ISBN 0-19-820744-1

Wikipedia

Luk Thep Doll

Thailand's Intriguing 'Luk Thep' Doll Culture | Time.com

time.com/4353544/thailand-luk-thep-doll

Thai Smile Airways lets people book seats for dolls | CNN ...

www.cnn.com/.../thai-smile-airways-luk-thep-doll/index.htm

Wikipedia

Nagoro, Japan

Rowthorn, Chris (2015). Japan (14th ed.). Footscray, Victoria: Lonely Planet.

Rao, Mallika (2014-05-06) [2014-05-01]. "In This Abandoned Japanese Village, The Life-Size Dolls Outnumber The People". Huffington Post.

McCurry, Justin (2015-01-07). "In ageing Japanese village, dolls take place of dwindling population". The Guardian.

Jaffe, Ina (2016-08-26). "A Dying Japanese Village Brought Back To Life — By Scarecrows". Morning Edition. NPR.

Grundhauser, Eric (2015-03-23). "Toys Are Us: The Japanese Village Where Dolls Outnumber People". Slate.

Souppouris, Aaron (2014-05-02). "Explore the hidden Japanese village where dolls replace the departed". The Verge.

Sim, David (2015-03-16). "Village of the scarecrows: Residents of Nagoro in Japan are being replaced by life-size straw dolls". international Business Times.

Schneider, Kate (2013-06-21). "Creepy or cool? Village of life-sized dolls in Nagoro, Japan". news.com.au.

Wikipedia

Isla De Las Munecas (Island of the Dolls)

Isla de las Munecas - Official Site

www.isladelasmunecas.com

Isla De Las Munecas Is The Island Of Decapitated Dolls ...

www.huffingtonpost.com/2014/08/14/islas-de-las-munecas

Wikipedia

Ghost Marriages

Baker, Hugh D. R. Chinese Family and Kinship. New York: Columbia University Press, 1979.

As quoted by Baker: Ball, J. Dyer, Things Chinese: or Notes Connected with China, London, 1904.

Freedman, Maurice. Family and Kinship in Chinese Society. Stanford, CA: Stanford university Press, 1970.

Ikels, Charlotte. "Parental Perspectives on the Significance of Marriage." Journal of Marriage and the Family Vol. 47 No. 2 (May 1985):253-264.

Jordan, David K. Gods, Ghosts, and Ancestors: The Folk Religion of a Taiwanese Village. Berkeley, Los Angeles, London: University of California Press, 1972.

The Cult of the Dead in a Chinese Village. Stanford, CA: Stanford University Press, 1973.

Stockard, Janice E. Daughters of the Canton Delta: Marriage Patterns and Economic Strategies in South China, 1860-1930.Stanford, CA: Stanford University Press, 1989.

Topley, Marjorie. "Ghost Marriages Among the Singapore Chinese." Man (Published by the Royal Anthropological Institute of Great Britain and Ireland) Vol. 55 (Feb., 1955): 29-30.

Topley, Marjorie. "Ghost Marriages Among the Singapore Chinese: A Further Note." Man (Published by the Royal Anthropological Institute of Great Britain and Ireland) Vol. 56 (May, 1956).

Wolf, Arthur P. Studies in Chinese Society. Stanford, CA: Stanford University Press, 1978.

Wolf, Arthur P., and Chieh-shan Huang. Marriage and Adoption in China, 1845-1945. Stanford, CA: Stanford University Press, 1980.

Wikipedia